LIBRETTO

The Gondoliers

or
The King Of Barataria

DRAMATIS PERSONAE

THE DUKE OF PLAZA-TORO *(a Grandee of Spain)*

LUIZ *(his Attendant)*

DON ALHAMBRA DEL BOLERO *(the Grand Inquisitor)*

MARCO PALMIERI
GIUSEPPE PALMIERI
ANTONIO
FRANCESCO } *(Venetian Gondoliers)*
GIORGIO
ANNIBALE

THE DUCHESS OF PLAZA-TORO

CASILDA *(her daughter)*

GIANETTA
TESSA
FIAMETTA } *(Contadine)*
VITTORIA
GIULIA

INEZ *(the King's Foster-mother)*

Chorus of Gondoliers and Contadine, Men-at-Arms, Heralds and Pages

ACT I—The Piazzetta, Venice
ACT II—Pavilion in the Palace of Barataria

(An interval of three months is supposed to elapse between Acts I and II)

*Time—*1750

MUSICAL NUMBERS

ACT I

No. *Page*

© 1993 International Music Publications Ltd
Griffin House, 161 Hammersmith Road,
London W6 8BS, England

Musical Numbers *(contd.)*

ACT II

OVERTURE

ACT I

SCENE—*The Piazetta, Venice. The Ducal Palace on the right.*

FIAMETTA, GIULIA, VITTORIA, *and other Contadine discovered, each tying a bouquet of roses.*

Music No. 1	CHORUS OF CONTADINE (Sopranos 1 & 2) with Solos *Gondoliers, Antonio, Mario and Giuseppe* "List And Learn"
CHORUS (Sopranos 1 & 2)	List and learn, list and learn, List and learn, ye dainty roses, Roses white and roses red, Why we bind you into posies Ere your morning bloom has fled. By a law of maiden's making, Accents of a heart that's aching, Even though that heart be breaking, Should by maiden be unsaid: Though they love with love exceeding, They must seem to be unheeding— Go ye then and do their pleading, Roses white and roses red! List and learn, List and learn, ye dainty roses, Roses white and roses red, Why we bind you into posies Ere your morning bloom has fled. List and learn, list and learn, Roses white and roses red, Roses, Oh list, list and learn, List and learn, Oh, roses white and red!
FIAMETTA	Two there are for whom, in duty, Ev'ry maid in Venice sighs— Two so peerless in their beauty That they shame the summer skies. We have hearts for them, in plenty, They have hearts, but all too few, We, alas, are four and twenty! They, alas, are only two! We alas,
CHORUS	Alas!
FIAMETTA	Are four and twenty! They, alas!

4

CHORUS	Alas!
FIAMETTA	Are only two!
CHORUS	They, alas, are only two! Alas!

Now ye know, ye dainty roses,
Roses white and roses red,
Why we bind you into posies
Ere your morning bloom has fled.
Now ye know, now ye know,
Roses white and roses red,
Roses, Oh now, now ye know,
Now ye know,
Oh roses white and red!

> *(During this chorus ANTONIO, FRANCESCO, GIORGIO, and other Gondoliers have entered unobserved by the Girls—at first two, then two more, then four, then half-a-dozen, then the remainder of the Chorus)*

FRANCESCO	Good morrow, pretty maids; for whom prepare ye These floral tributes extraordinary?
FIAMETTA	For Marco and Giuseppe Palmieri, The pink and flower of all the Gondolieri.
GIULIA	They're coming here, as we have heard but lately, To choose two brides from us who sit sedately.
ANTONIO	Do all you maidens love them?
ALL (GIRLS)	Passionately!
ANTONIO	These gondoliers are to be envied greatly!
GIORGIO	But what of us, who one and all adore you? Have pity on our passion, we implore you!
FIAMETTA	These gentlemen must make their choice before you;
VITTORIA	In the meantime we tacitly ignore you.
GIULIA	When they have chosen two that leaves you plenty— Two dozen we, and ye are four-and-twenty.
FIA. & VIT.	Till then, enjoy your *dolce far niente*.
ANTONIO	With pleasure, nobody *contradicente!* For the merriest fellows are we,
CHORUS (GIRLS & MEN)	Tra la, tra la, tra la,
ANT. & CHOR.	Tra la la la la, Tra la la la,
ANTONIO	That ply on the emerald sea,
CHORUS	Tra la, tra la, tra la,
ANT. & CHOR.	Tra la la la la, Tra la la la.

ANTONIO	With loving and laughing, And quipping and quaffing, We're happy as happy can be,
CHORUS	Tra la!
ANTONIO	With loving and laughing And quipping and quaffing, We're happy as happy can be!
CHORUS	Tra la la la la la la la, Tra la la la, tra la la la,
ANT. & CHOR.	Tra la la la la la la la, Tra la, tra la, la la,

ANTONIO		**CHORUS**	
Tra la la la la la la, Tra la la la la la, Tra la la la, La la la la,			La la la la la la la la, La la la la la la la la, La la la la, La la la la,

ALL	La la la la la la, la la la la la la la, Tra la!
ANTONIO	With sorrow we've nothing to do,
CHORUS	Tra la, tra la, tra la,
ANT. & CHOR.	Tra la la la la, Tra la la la,
ANTONIO	And care is a thing to pooh-pooh,
CHORUS	Tra la, tra la, tra la,
ANT. & CHOR.	Tra la la la la, Tra la la la,
ANTONIO	And Jealousy yellow, Unfortunate fellow, We drown in the shimmering blue,
CHORUS	Tra la!
ANTONIO	And Jealousy yellow, Unfortunate fellow, We drown in the shimmering blue!
CHORUS	Tra la la la la la la la, Tra la la la, tra la la la,
ANT. & CHOR.	Tra la la la la la la la, Tra la, tra la, la la,

ANTONIO		**CHORUS**	
Tra la la la la la la, Tra la la la la la, Tra la la la, La la la la,			La la la la la la la la, La la la la la la la la, La la la la, La la la la,

ALL	La la la la la la, la la la la la la la, Tra la!
FIAMETTA	*(looking off)* See, see, at last they come to make their choice— Let us acclaim them with united voice.

(MARCO and GIUSEPPE appear in gondola at back)

CHORUS *(Girls)* Hail, hail, gallant gondolieri, ben' venuti! Ben' venuti!
Accept our love, our homage and our duty.
Ben' venuti! ben' venuti!

(MARCO and GIUSEPPE jump ashore—the girls salute them)

MAR. & GIUS. Buon' giorno, signorine!

GIRLS Gondolieri carissimi!
Siamo contadine!

MAR. & GIUS. *(bowing)* Servitori umilissimi!
Per chi questi fiori—
Questi fiori bellissimi?

GIRLS Per voi, bei signori,
O eccellentissimi!

(The girls present their bouquets to MARCO and GIUSEPPE, who are overwhelmed with them, and carry them with difficulty.)

MAR. & GIUS. *(their arms full of flowers)* O ciel! O ciel!

GIRLS Buon' giorno, cavalieri!

MAR. & GIUS. *(deprecatingly)* Siamo gondolieri,
(To FIA. & VIT.) Signorina, io t'amo!

GIRLS *(deprecatingly)* Contadine siamo.

MEN Signorine!

GIRLS *(deprecatingly)* Contadine!
(Curtseying to MAR. & GIUS.) Cavalieri.

MEN Gondolieri!

MAR. & GIUS. *(deprecatingly)* Poveri gondolieri!

MAR., GIUS. & MEN Poveri gondolieri!
Buon' giorno, signorine!

GIRLS Gondolieri carissimi!
Siamo contadine!

MAR., GIUS. & MEN Servitori umilissimi!

MARCO	Per	**MEN**	Servi-
	noi		tori
	questi		umi-
	fior-		lissi-
	i-Questi		mi! Servi-
	fior-		tori
	i bellissimi!		umilissimi,
1st SOPRANOS	Per	**MEN**	Servi-
	voi		tori

7

1st SOPRANOS (*Contd.*)	Bei si- gno- ri, O eccellen- — tissimi!	**MEN** (*Contd.*)	umi- lissi- mi, umi- lis- si- mi,

MAR., GIUS. & MEN   Signorine!

GIRLS   Contadine! Cavalieri!

MAR., GIUS. & MEN   Gondolieri!

ALL   Buon' giorno, {Signorine! / Cavalieri!}

MAR. & GIUS.
We're called *gondolieri*, but that's a vagary,
It's quite honorary
The trade that we ply.
For gallantry noted since we were short-coated
To beauty devoted.
Giuseppe }
Are Marco } and I
When morning is breaking, our couches forsaking,
To greet their awaking
With carols we come.
At summer day's nooning, when weary lagooning,

MARCO		**GIUSEPPE**	
	Our man- dolins tu- ning, We la- zi- ly— thrum. Tra la la la la, Tra la la la la, Tra la la la la, Tra la la la la, Tra la la la la, Tra la la la la, Tra la la la la, Tra la la la la,		Our mandolins tu- ning, We lazily thrum, Our mandolins tuning, We lazi- ly, lazily thrum. Our man- do- lins tu- ning, We la- zi- ly thrum.

BOTH
Tra la la la la la la,
Tra la la la la la la,
Tra la la la la,
Tra la la la la!
When vespers are ringing, to hope ever clinging,
With songs of our singing
A vigil we keep.
When daylight is fading, enwrapt in night's shading,
With soft serenading
We sing them to sleep.

MARCO		GIUSEPPE
With soft se-re-na-		We sing
—		them, We sing them to sleep.
ding, We sing them to sleep,		With soft serenading
With soft serenading		We sing them to sleep.
We sing them to sleep.		
We're		
call'd		Tra la
—		la la la, Tra la la
gon-		la la,
do-lier-		Tra la la la la,
i,		Tra la la la
But		la,
that's		Tra la la la la,
a		Tra la la la
va-		la la!
ga-ry.		

BOTH

Gondolieri, Gondolieri,
Tra la la la la,
Tra la la la la la la!
Gondolieri, Gondolieri,
Tra la la la la,
Tra la la la la,
Tra la la la la,
Tra la la la la,
Tra la la la la,
Tra la!

RECITATIVE—MARCO *and* GIUSEPPE.

MARCO   And now to choose our brides!

GIUSEPPE   As all are young and fair, and amiable besides,

BOTH   We really do not care a pref'rence to declare.

MARCO   A bias to disclose would be indelicate—

GIUSEPPE   And therefore we propose to let impartial Fate
Select for us a mate!

ALL   Viva!

GIRLS   A bias to disclose would be indelicate—

MEN   But how do they propose
To let impartial Fate select for them a mate?

GIUSEPPE   These handkerchiefs upon our eyes be good enough to bind,

MARCO   And take good care that both of us are absolutely blind;

BOTH   Then turn us round—and we, with all convenient despatch,
Will undertake to marry any two of you we catch!

ALL   Viva!

They undertake to marry any two of { us they catch! / them they catch! }

(The girls prepare to bind their eyes as directed)

FIAMETTA	*(to MARCO)* Are you peeping? Can you see me?
MARCO	Dark I'm keeping, dark and dreamy!

(MARCO slyly lifts bandage)

VITTORIA	*(to GIUSEPPE)* If you're blinded, truly say so,
GIUSEPPE	All right-minded players play so!

(Slyly lifts bandage)

FIAMETTA	*(detecting MARCO)* Conduct shady! They are cheating! Surely they deserve a beating!

(Replaces bandage)

VITTORIA	*(detecting GIUSEPPE)* This too much is; maidens mocking; Conduct such is truly shocking!

(Replaces bandage)

CHORUS (Girls)
You can
spy, sir! Shut
your
eye, sir! You can
spy, sir! Shut
your
eye, sir! You may
use it by-
and-
by, sir!

You can see, sir! Don't tell
me, sir! You can see, sir! Don't tell
me, sir! That will do—now let it
be, sir! That will do—now let it
be, sir!

CHORUS (Men)
Fie,
for
shame,
Fie,
for
shame,
Fie,
for
shame!
You can
see, sir! Don't tell me, sir!
You can see, sir! Don't tell me, sir!
That will do—now let it be, sir!
That will do—now let it, let it
be, sir!

CHORUS (Girls)	My papa he keeps three horses, Black, and white, and dapple grey, sir; Turn three times, then take your courses, Catch whichever girl you may, sir!
CHORUS (Men)	My papa he keeps three horses, Black, and white, and dapple grey, sir; Turn three times, then take your courses, Catch whichever girl you may, sir.
GIRLS & MEN	My papa he keeps three horses, Black, and white, and dapple grey, sir.

MARCO and GIUSEPPE turn round, as directed, and try to catch the girls. Business of blind-man's buff. Eventually MARCO catches GIANETTA, and GIUSEPPE catches TESSA. The two girls try to escape, but in vain. The two men pass their hands over the girls' faces to discover their identity.

GIUSEPPE	*(guessing)* I've at length achieved a capture! This is Tessa! *(removes bandage)* Rapture, rapture!

CHORUS	Rapture, rapture!	
MARCO	*(guessing)* To me Gianetta fate has granted! *(removes bandage)* Just the very girl I wanted!	
CHORUS	Just the very girl he wanted!	
GIUSEPPE	*(politely to MARCO)* If you'd rather change—	
TESSA	My goodness! This indeed is simple rudeness.	
MARCO	*(politely to GIUSEPPE)* I've no preference whatever—	
GIANETTA	Listen to him! Well, I never!	

(Each man kisses each girl)

GIANETTA   Thank you gallant *gondolieri*! In a set and formal measure
It is scarcely necessary
To express our pleasure. Each of us to prove a treasure,
Conjugal and monetary,
Gladly will devote our leisure, gallant *gondolieri*,
Tra la, la, la, la, la, Tra la, la, la, la, la, la,
Tra la, la, la, la, la, la, la, la, la, la, la, la, la,
La la!

TESSA   Gay and gallant *gondolieri*, take us both and hold us tightly,
You have luck extr'ordinary;
We might have been unsightly! If we judge your conduct rightly,
'Twas a choice involuntary;
Still we thank you most politely, gay and gallant *gondolieri*!
Tra la, la, la, la, la, la, Tra la, la, la, la, la, la,
Tra la, la, la, la, la, la, la, la, la, la, la, la, la,
La la!

CHORUS   Tra la, la, la, la, la, la, la, la, la!

1st SOPRANOS	2nd SOPRANOS & TENORS	BASSES
Thank		La,
	La,	
you,		
	la,	
gal-		la,
	la,	
lant		
	la,	
gon-		la,
	la,	
do-		
	la,	
lier-		la,
	la,	
i:		
	la,	
In		la,
	la,	
a		
	la,	
set		la,

1st SOPRANOS *(Contd.)*	2nd SOPRANOS & TENORS *(Contd.)*	BASSES *(Contd.)*
	la,	
and	la,	
for-	la,	la,
mal	la,	
mea-	la,	la,
sure,	la,	
It	la,	la,
is	la,	
scarce-	la,	la,
ly	la,	
ne-	la,	la,
ces-	la,	
sa-	la,	la,
ry	la,	
To	la,	la,
ex-	la,	
press	la,	la,
our	la,	
plea-	la,	la,
—	la,	
sure.	la,	la,
Each	la, la,	la,
of	la,	
us	la,	la,
to	la,	
prove	la,	la,
a	la,	
trea-	la,	la,
sure,	la,	
	la,	

1st SOPRANOS *(Contd.)*	2nd SOPRANOS & TENORS *(Contd.)*	BASSES *(Contd.)*
Glad-		la,
	la,	
ly	la,	
will		la,
	la,	
de-	la,	
vote		la,
	la,	
our	la,	
lei-		la,
	la,	
sure,		
	la,	
Gay and	la, la,	la, la,
	la,	la,
gal-lant	la, la,	la, la,
	la,	la,
gon-do-	la, la,	la, la,
	la,	la,
lier-i.	la, la,	la, la,
	la,	la,

1st & 2nd SOPRANOS	TENORS & BASSES
Tra la la la, Tra la la la la la la la! Tra la la la, la la!	Tra la la la, Tra la la la! Tra la la la, la la!

GIAN., TESSA & 1st & 2nd SOPRANOS	
Fate in this has put his finger— Let us bow to Fate's decree,	Fate in this has put his finger— Let us bow to Fate's decree, Then
Then no longer let us linger, To the altar hurry we! Tra la la la la la la la la la la!	no longer let us linger, To the altar hurry we! Tra la la la la la la la la la la!

(They all dance off two and two—GIANETTA with MARCO, TESSA with GIUSEPPE)

Flourish. A gondola arrives at the Piazzetta steps, from which enter the DUKE OF PLAZA-TORO, the DUCHESS, their daughter CASILDA, and their attendant LUIZ, who carries a drum. All are dressed in pompous but old and faded clothes.

Music No. 2	*Entrance of* DUKE, DUCHESS, CASILDA *and* LUIZ. "From The Sunny Spanish Shore"
DUKE	From the sunny Spanish shore, The Duke of Plaza-Tor'—

DUCHESS	And His Grace's Duchess true—
CASILDA	And His Grace's daughter, too—
LUIZ	And his Grace's private drum To Venetia's shores have come, To Venetia's shores have come.
ALL	And if ever, ever, ever they get back to Spain, They will never, never, never cross the sea again— They will never, never, never, never, Never, never, never, never, Never, never, never cross the sea again.
DUKE	Neither that Grandee from the Spanish shore, The noble Duke of Plaza Tor'—
DUCHESS	Nor His Grace's Duchess, staunch and true—
CASILDA	You may add, His Grace's daughter, too—
LUIZ	Nor His Grace's own particular drum To Venetia's shores will come. To Venetia's shores will come!

ALL	If ever, ever, ever they get back to Spain,
	They will never, never, never cross the sea again!
	They will never, never, never, never, never, never, never, never, never,
	    never, never cross the sea again.
	They will never, never, never, never, never, never, never, never, never,
	    never, never cross the sea again.

DUKE	At last we have arrived at our destination. This is the Ducal Palace, and it is here that the Grand Inquisitor resides. As a Castilian hidalgo of ninety-five quarterings, I regret that I am unable to pay my state visit on a horse. As a Castilian hidalgo of that description, I should have preferred to ride through the streets of Venice; but owing, I presume, to an unusually wet season, the streets are in such a condition that equestrian exercise is impracticable. No matter. Where is our suite?
LUIZ	*(coming forward)* Your Grace, I am here.
DUCHESS	Why do you not do yourself the honour to kneel when you address His Grace?
DUKE	My love, it is so small a matter! *(To LUIZ)* Still, you may as well do it. *(LUIZ kneels)*
CASILDA	The young man seems to entertain but an imperfect appreciation of the respect due from a menial to a Castilian hidalgo.
DUKE	My child, you are hard upon our suite.
CASILDA	Papa, I've no patience with the presumption of persons in his plebeian position. If he does not appreciate that position, let him be whipped until he does.
DUKE	Let us hope the omission was not intended as a slight. I should be much hurt if I thought it was. So would he. *(To LUIZ)* Where are the halberdiers who were to have had the honour of meeting us here, that our visit to the Grand Inquisitor might be made in becoming state?

LUIZ	Your Grace, the halberdiers are mercenary people who stipulated for a trifle on account.
DUKE	How tiresome! Well, let us hope the Grand Inquisitor is a blind gentleman. And the band who were to have had the honour of escorting us? I see no band!
LUIZ	Your Grace, the band are sordid persons who required to be paid in advance.
DUCHESS	That's so like a band!
DUKE	*(annoyed)* Insuperable difficulties meet me at every turn!
DUCHESS	But surely they know His Grace?
LUIZ	Exactly—they know His Grace.
DUKE	Well, let us hope that the Grand Inquisitor is a deaf gentleman. A cornet-à-piston would be something. You do not happen to possess the accomplishment of tootling like a cornet-à-piston?
LUIZ	Alas no, your Grace! But I can imitate a farmyard.
DUKE	*(doubtfully)* I don't see how that would help us. I don't see how we could bring it in.
CASILDA	It would not help us in the least. We are not a parcel of graziers come to market, dolt! *(LUIZ rises)*
DUKE	My love, our suite's feelings! *(To LUIZ)* Be so good as to ring the bell and inform the Grand Inquisitor that his Grace the Duke of Plaza-Toro, Count Matadoro, Baron Picadoro—
DUCHESS	And suite—
DUKE	And suite—have arrived in Venice, and seek—
CASILDA	Desire—
DUCHESS	Demand!
DUKE	And demand an audience.
LUIZ	Your Grace has but to command.
DUKE	*(much moved)* I felt sure of it—I felt sure of it! *(Exit LUIZ into Ducal Palace)* And now, my love—*(aside to DUCHESS)* Shall we tell her? I think so— *(aloud to CASILDA)* And now, my love, prepare for a magnificent surprise. It is my agreeable duty to reveal to you a secret which should make you the happiest young lady in Venice!
CASILDA	A secret?
DUCHESS	A secret which, for State reasons, it has been necessary to preserve for twenty years.
DUKE	When you were a prattling babe of six months old you were married by proxy to no less a personage than the infant son and heir of His Majesty the immeasurably wealthy King of Barataria!

15

CASILDA	Married to the infant son of the King of Barataria? Was I consulted? *(DUKE shakes his head)* Then it was a most unpardonable liberty!
DUKE	Consider his extreme youth and forgive him. Shortly after the ceremony that misguided monarch abandoned the creed of his forefathers and became a Wesleyan Methodist of the most bigoted and persecuting type. The Grand Inquisitor, determined that the innovation should not be perpetuated in Barataria, caused your smiling and unconscious husband to be stolen and conveyed to Venice. A fortnight since the Methodist Monarch and all his Wesleyan Court were killed in an insurrection, and we are here to ascertain the whereabouts of your husband, and to hail you, our daughter, as Her Majesty, the reigning Queen of Barataria! *(Kneels)*

(During this speech LUIZ re-enters)

DUCHESS	Your Majesty! *(Kneels)*

(Drum roll)

DUKE	It is at such moments as these that one feels how necessary it is to travel with a full band.
CASILDA	I, the Queen of Barataria! But I've nothing to wear! We are practically penniless!
DUKE	That point has not escaped me. Although I am unhappily in straitened circumstances at present, my social influence is something enormous; and a Company, to be called the Duke of Plaza-Toro, Limited, is in course of formation to work me. An influential directorate has been secured, and I shall myself join the Board after allotment.
CASILDA	Am I to understand that the Queen of Barataria may be called upon at any time to witness her honoured sire in process of liquidation?
DUCHESS	The speculation is not exempt from that drawback. If your father should stop, it will, of course, be necessary to wind him up.
CASILDA	But it's so undignified—it's so degrading! A Grandee of Spain turned into a public company! Such a thing was never heard of!
DUKE	My child, the Duke of Plaza-Toro does not follow fashions—he leads them. He always leads everybody. When he was in the army he led his regiment. He occasionally led them into action. He invariably led them out of it.
Music No. 3	SONG (Duke of Plaza-Toro) *with* Duchess, Casilda *and* Luiz. "In Enterprise Of Martial Kind"
DUKE	In enterprise of martial kind, When there was any fighting, He led his regiment from behind— He found it less exciting. But when away his regiment ran, His place was at the fore, O— That celebrated, cultivated, underrated Nobleman, The Duke of Plaza-Toro!

ALL	In the first and foremost flight, ha, ha! You always found that knight, ha, ha! That celebrated, cultivated, underrated Nobleman, The Duke of Plaza-Toro!
DUKE	When, to evade Destruction's hand, To hide they all proceeded, No soldier in that gallant band Hid half as well as he did. He lay conceal'd throughout the war, And so preserv'd his gore, O! That unaffected, undetected, well-connected Warrior, The Duke of Plaza-Toro!
ALL	In ev'ry doughty deed, ha, ha! He always took the lead, ha, ha! That unaffected, undetected, well-connected Warrior, The Duke of Plaza-Toro!
DUKE	When told that they would all be shot Unless they left the service, That hero hesitated not, So marvellous his nerve is. He sent his resignation in, The first of all his corps, O! That very knowing, overflowing, easy-going Paladin, The Duke of Plaza-Toro!
ALL	To men of grosser clay, ha, ha! He always showed the way, ha, ha! That very knowing, overflowing, easy-going Paladin, The Duke of Plaza-Toro! That very knowing, overflowing, easy-going Paladin, The Duke of Plaza-Toro!

(Exeunt DUKE and DUCHESS into Grand Ducal Palace. As soon as they have disappeared, LUIZ and CASILDA rush to each other's arms)

Music No. 4	RECITATIVE and DUET (Casilda *and* Luiz) "O Rapture, When Alone Together"
BOTH	O rapture, when alone together Two loving hearts and those that bear them May join in temporary tether, Though Fate apart should rudely tear them,
CASILDA	Necessity, Invention's mother, Compell'd me to a course of feigning— But, left alone with one another, I will atone for my disdaining! Ah, well beloved, Mine angry frown

CASILDA *(Contd.)*　Is but a gown
That serves to dress
My gentleness!

LUIZ　Ah, well beloved,
Thy cold disdain,
It gives no pain—
'Tis mercy, played
In masquerade!
Ah, well beloved!

CASILDA	**LUIZ**
Ah, well belov-	
Ah, well belov-	
ed!	Ah, well belov-
Ah, well belov-	ed!
ed!	Ah, well belov-
Mine	ed! Thine
angry frown	angry frown
Is but a gown	Is but a gown
That serves to dress	That serves to dress
My gentleness!	Thy gentleness!
	Ah, belov-
Ah,	—
well	ed!
Ah, well beloved, beloved!	Ah, well beloved, beloved!

CASILDA　O Luiz, Luiz—what have you said! What have I done! What have I allowed you to do!

LUIZ　Nothing, I trust, that you will ever have reason to repent. *(Offering to embrace her)*

CASILDA　*(withdrawing from him)* Nay, Luiz, it may not be. I have embraced you for the last time.

LUIZ　*(amazed)* Casilda!

CASILDA　I have just learnt, to my surprise and indignation, that I was wed in babyhood to the infant son of the King of Barataria!

LUIZ　The son of the King of Barataria? The child who was stolen in infancy by the Inquisition?

CASILDA　The same. But, of course, you know his story.

LUIZ　Know his story? Why, I have often told you that my mother was the nurse to whose charge he was entrusted!

CASILDA　True. I had forgotten. Well, he has been discovered, and my father has brought me here to claim his hand.

LUIZ　But you will not recognize this marriage? It took place when you were too young to understand its import.

CASILDA　Nay, Luiz, respect my principles and cease to torture me with vain entreaties. Henceforth my life is another's.

LUIZ　But stay—the present and the future—*they* are another's; but the past— that at least is ours, and none can take it from us. As we may revel in naught else, let us revel in that!

CASILDA	I don't think I grasp your meaning.
LUIZ	Yet it is logical enough. You say you cease to love me?
CASILDA	*(demurely)* I say I *may* not love you.
LUIZ	Ah, but you do not say you *did* not love me?
CASILDA	I loved you with a frenzy that words are powerless to express—and that but ten brief minutes since!
LUIZ	Exactly. My own—that is, until ten minutes since, my own—my lately loved, my recently adored—tell me that until, say a quarter of an hour ago, I was all in all to thee! *(Embracing her)*
CASILDA	I see your idea. It's ingenious, but don't do that.

(Releasing herself)

LUIZ	There can be no harm in revelling in the past.
CASILDA	None whatever, but an embrace cannot be taken to act retrospectively.
LUIZ	Perhaps not! Ah, Casilda, you were to me as the sun is to the earth!
CASILDA	And now our love, so full of life, is but a silent, solemn memory!
LUIZ	Must it be so, Casilda?
CASILDA	Luiz, it must be so!

Music No. 5	<div align="center">DUET (Casilda *and* Luiz) "There Was A Time"</div>
LUIZ	There was a time— A time for ever gone—ah, woe is me! It was no crime To love but thee alone—ah, woe is me! One heart, one life, one soul, One aim, one goal— Each in the other's thrall, Each all in all, ah, woe is me! Ah, woe is me!
BOTH	Oh, bury, bury—let the grave close o'er The days that were—that never will be more! Oh, bury, bury love that all condemn, And let the whirlwind mourn its requiem!
CASILDA	Dead as the last year's leaves— As gather'd flowers—ah, woe is me! Dead as the garner'd sheaves, That love of ours—ah, woe is me! Born but to fade and die When hope was high, Dead and as far away As yesterday!—ah, woe is me!
BOTH	Oh, bury, bury—let the grave close o'er The days that were—that never will be more!

BOTH *(Contd.)*	Oh, bury, bury love that all condemn, And let the whirlwind mourn its requiem, Its requiem, its requiem!
	(Re-enter from the Ducal Palace the DUKE and DUCHESS, followed by DON ALHAMBRA DEL BOLERO, the Grand Inquisitor)
DUKE	My child, allow me to present to you His Distinction Don Alhambra del Bolero, the Grand Inquisitor of Spain. It was His Distinction who so thoughtfully abstracted your infant husband and brought him to Venice.
DON AL.	So this is the little lady who is so unexpectedly called upon to assume the functions of Royalty! And a very nice little lady, too!
DUKE	Jimp, isn't she?
DON AL.	Distinctly jimp. Allow me. *(Offers his hand. She turns away scornfully)* Naughty temper!
DUKE	You must make some allowance. Her Majesty's head is a little turned by her access of dignity.
DON AL.	I could have wished that Her Majesty's access of dignity had turned it in this direction.
DUCHESS	Unfortunately, if I am not mistaken, there appears to be some little doubt as to His Majesty's whereabouts.
CASILDA	*(aside)* A doubt as to his whereabouts? Then we may yet be saved!
DON AL.	A doubt? Oh dear no—no doubt at all! He is here, in Venice, plying the modest but picturesque calling of a gondolier. I can give you his address—I see him every day! In the entire annals of our history there is absolutely no circumstance so entirely free from all manner of doubt of any kind whatever! Listen, and I'll tell you all about it.
Music No. 6	SONG—Don Alhambra *(with* Duke, Duchess, Casilda *and* Luiz*)* "I Stole the Prince"
DON AL.	I stole the Prince, and I brought him here. And left him gaily prattling With a highly respectable gondolier, Who promised the Royal babe to rear, And teach him the trade of a timoneer With his own beloved bratling. Both of the babes were strong and stout, And considering all things, clever, Of that there is no manner of doubt— No probable possible shadow of doubt— No possible doubt whatever.
ALL *except* **DON AL.**	No possible doubt whatever!
DON AL.	But owing, I'm much disposed to fear, To his terrible taste for tippling, That highly respectable gondolier Could never declare with a mind sincere Which of the two was his offspring dear, And which the Royal stripling!

DON AL. *(Contd.)*   Which was which he could never make out
Despite his best endeavour.
Of *that* there is no manner of doubt—
No probable, possible shadow of doubt—
No possible doubt whatever.

ALL *except* **DON AL.**   No possible doubt whatever!

DON AL.   Time sped, and when at the end of a year
I sought that infant cherished,
That highly respectable gondolier
Was lying a corpse on his humble bier—
I dropp'd a Grand Inquisitor's tear—
That gondolier had perished.

A taste for drink, combined with gout,
Had doubled him up for ever.
Of *that* there is no manner of doubt—
No probable, possible shadow of doubt—
No possible doubt whatever.

ALL *except* **DON AL.**   No possible doubt whatever!

DON AL.   The children followed his old career—
(This statement can't be parried)
Of a highly respectable gondolier:
Well, one of the two (who will soon be here)—
But *which* of the two it is not quite clear—
Is the Royal Prince you married!

Search in and out and round about
And you'll discover never
A tale so free from every doubt—
All probable, possible shadow of doubt—
All possible doubt whatever!

ALL *except* **DON AL.**   A tale so free from ev'ry doubt,
All probable, possible shadow of doubt—
All possible doubt whatever!

CASILDA   Then do you mean to say that I am married to one of two gondoliers, but it is impossible to say which?

DON AL.   Without any doubt of any kind whatever. But be reassured: the nurse to whom your husband was entrusted is the mother of the musical young man who is such a past-master of that delicately modulated instrument *(indicating the drum)*. She can, no doubt, establish the King's identity beyond all question.

LUIZ   Heavens, how did he know that?

DON AL.   My young friend, a Grand Inquisitor is always up to date. *(To CASILDA)* His mother is at present the wife of a highly respectable and old-established brigand, who carries on an extensive practice in the mountains around Cordova. Accompanied by two of my emissaries, he will set off at once for his mother's address. She will return with them, and if she finds any difficulty in making up her mind, the persuasive influence of the torture chamber will jog her memory.

21

RECITATIVE (Casilda *and* Don Alhambra)
"But Bless My Heart"

CASILDA

But, bless my heart, consider my position!
I am the wife of one, that's very clear;
But who can tell, except by intuition,
Which is the Prince, and which the Gondolier?

DON AL.

Submit to Fate without unseemly wrangle:
Such complications frequently occur—
Life is one closely complicated tangle:
Death is the only true unraveller!

QUINTET (Duke, Duchess, Casilda, Luiz *and* Grand Inquisitor)
"Try We Lifelong"

ALL

Try we life-long, we can never
Straighten out life's tangled skein,
Why should we, in vain endeavour,
Guess and guess and guess again?

LUIZ

Life's a pudding full of plums,

DUCHESS

Care's a canker that benumbs.

ALL

Life's a pudding full of plums,
Care's a canker that benumbs.
Wherefore waste our elocution
On impossible solution?
Life's a pleasant institution,
Let us take it as it comes,
Let us take it as it comes!

Set aside the dull enigma,
We shall guess it all too soon;

CASILDA	DUCHESS	LUIZ	DUKE & INQUISITOR
Failure			
brings no	Failure	Failure	Failure
kind of stigma	brings,	brings no kind of	brings no kind of
Dance	Failure	stig-	stig-
we		—	—
to an-	brings	ma-	—
other	no		ma-
tune!	kind		Dance we
	of		
	stigma-	Dance	to an-
Dance we	—	we	—
to an-	Dance	to an-	o-
other	we	o-	ther—
tune!—	to an-	ther	—
—	other tune!	tune!	tune!
	String	String the	String the
	the—	lyre and	lyre
	—	fill the	and
String the	lyre—	cup—	fill the
lyre and	—		cup, —
fill the	and		—
cup,	fill	Lest on	Lest on

CASILDA (Contd.)	DUCHESS (Contd.)	LUIZ (Contd.)	DUKE & INQUISITOR (Contd.)
	the—	sorrow	sor-
	—	we should	row
Lest on	cup,	sup,	we should—
sorrow	fill	we	sup, —
we should	the	should	—
sup,	cup,	sup,	

ALL

String the lyre, fill the cup
Lest on sorrow we should sup.
Hop and skip to Fancy's fiddle,
Hands across and down the middle—
Life's perhaps the only riddle
That we shrink from giving up!
Life's perhaps the only riddle
That we shrink from giving up!
Then take it as it comes,
Take it as it comes,
String the lyre, fill the cup
Lest on sorrow we should sup!
Take life as it comes!

(Exeunt all into Ducal Palace, except LUIZ, who goes off in gondola)

(Enter Gondoliers and Contadine, followed by MARCO, GIANETTA, GIUSEPPE and TESSA)

Music No. 9 CHORUS with Solo (Tessa)
"Bridegroom and Bride"

CHORUS (Girls)
Bridegroom and bride!
Knot that's insoluble   **MEN** Ah — — — — — — — —
Voices all voluble   — — — — — — — — —
Hail it with pride.   — — — — — — — — —

CHORUS (Girls)
Bridegroom and bride!
We in sincerity,   **MEN** Ah — — — — — — — —
Wish you prosperity,   — — — — — — — — —
Bridegroom and bride!   — — — — — — — — —

CHORUS
We in sincerity,
Wish you prosperity,
Bridegroom and bride!
Bridegroom and bride!

SONG: TESSA

TESSA
When a merry maiden marries,
Sorrow goes and pleasure tarries;
Ev'ry sound becomes a song,
All is right, and nothing's wrong!
From to-day and ever after
Let our tears be tears of laughter.
Ev'ry sigh that finds a vent
Be a sigh of sweet content!
When you marry merry maiden,
Then the air with love is laden;
Ev'ry flow'r is a rose,
Ev'ry goose becomes a swan,
Ev'ry kind of trouble goes
Where the last year's snows have gone!

TESSA	1st SOPRANOS	2nd SOPRANOS, TENORS & BASSES
Sunlight takes the	Sun-	Sun-
place of	light	light
shade	takes the place of shade	takes the place of shade
When you marry	When	When
merry	you	you
maid! —	marry merry maid!	marry merry maid!
—	When a merry	When
—	maiden	a
	marries, —	mer-
	—	ry
	Sorrow goes and	mai-
	pleasure	den
	tarries; —	mar-
	—	ries
Ev'ry sound be-	Ev'ry sound be-	Ev'ry sound's
comes a	comes a	a
song,	song,	song,
All is right and	All is right and	All is right and
nothing's wrong!	nothing's wrong!	nothing's wrong!

TESSA

When a merry maiden marries
Sorrow goes and pleasure tarries;
Ev'ry sound becomes a song—
All is right, and nothing's wrong!
Gnawing Care and aching Sorrow
Get ye gone until tomorrow;
Jealousies in grim array,
Ye are things of yesterday!
When you marry merry maiden,
Then the air with joy is laden;
All the corners of the earth
Ring with music sweetly played,
Worry is melodious mirth,
Grief is joy in masquerade;

TESSA	GIRLS	MEN
Sullen night is	Sul-	Sul-
laughing	len	len
day—	night is laughing day—	night is laughing day—
—	All the year is	All
	merry	the
	May! —	year is
Ah—	—	merry May!
All the year is	All	All
merry	is	is
May, —	merry	merry
All the year is	May,	May,
merry May!		
Merry, merry	Merry May,	Merry May,
May,		
merry, merry	merry May,	merry May,
May,		
All the year is merry,		
merry	is	is
May!	May!	May!

(At the end of the song, DON ALHAMBRA enters at back. The Gondoliers and Contadine shrink from him, and gradually go off, much alarmed)

24

GIUSEPPE	And now our lives are going to begin in real earnest! What's a bachelor? A mere nothing—he's a chrysalis. He can't be said to live—he exists.
MARCO	What a delightful institution marriage is! Why have we wasted all this time? Why didn't we marry ten years ago?
TESSA	Because you couldn't find anybody nice enough.
GIANETTA	Because you were waiting for *us*.
MARCO	I suppose that *was* the reason. We were waiting for you without knowing it. *(DON ALHAMBRA comes forward)* Hallo!
DON AL.	Good morning.
GIUSEPPE	If this gentleman is an undertaker, it's a bad omen.
DON AL.	Ceremony of some sort going on?
GIUSEPPE	*(aside)* He *is* an undertaker! *(Aloud)* No—a little unimportant family gathering. Nothing in *your* line.
DON AL.	Somebody's birthday, I suppose?
GIANETTA	Yes, mine!
TESSA	And mine!
MARCO	And mine!
GIUSEPPE	And mine!
DON AL.	Curious coincidence! And how old may you all be?
TESSA	It's a rude question—but about ten minutes.
DON AL.	Remarkably fine children! But surely you are jesting?
TESSA	In other words, we were married about ten minutes since.
DON AL.	Married! You don't mean to say you are married?
MARCO	Oh yes, we are married.
DON AL.	What, both of you?
ALL	All four of us.
DON AL.	*(aside)* Bless my heart, how extremely awkward!
GIANETTA	You don't mind, I suppose?
TESSA	You were not thinking of either of us for yourself, I presume? Oh, Giuseppe, look at him—he was. He's heartbroken!
DON AL.	Oh, no, I wasn't! I wasn't!
GIUSEPPE	Now, my man *(slapping him on the back)*, we don't want anything in your line to-day, and if your curiosity's satisfied—you can go!

DON AL.	You mustn't call me your man. It's a liberty. I don't think you know who I am.
GIUSEPPE	Not we, indeed! We are jolly gondoliers, the sons of Baptisto Palmieri, who led the last revolution. Republicans, heart and soul, we hold all men to be equal. As we abhor oppression, we abhor kings: as we detest vain-glory, we detest rank: as we despise effeminacy, we despise wealth. We are Venetian gondoliers—your equals in everything except our calling, and in that at once your masters and your servants.
DON AL.	Bless my heart, how unfortunate! One of you may be Baptisto's son, for anything I know to the contrary; but the other is no less a personage than the only son of the late King of Barataria.
ALL	What!
DON AL.	And I trust—I *trust* it was that one who slapped me on the shoulder and called me his man!
GIUSEPPE	One of us a king!
MARCO	Not brothers!
TESSA	The King of Barataria!
GIANETTA	Well, who'd have thought it!
MARCO	But which is it?
DON AL.	What does it matter? As you are both Republicans, and hold kings in detestation, of course you'll abdicate at once. Good morning! *(Going)*
GIA. & TESSA	Oh, don't do that! *(MARCO and GIUSEPPE stop him)*
GIUSEPPE	Well, as to that, of course, there are kings and kings. When I say that I detest kings, I mean I detest *bad* kings.
DON AL.	I see. It's a delicate distinction.
GIUSEPPE	Quite so. Now I can conceive a kind of king—an ideal king—the creature of my fancy, you know—who would be absolutely unobjectionable. A king, for instance, who would abolish taxes and make everything cheap, except gondolas—
MARCO	And give a great many free entertainments to the gondoliers—
GIUSEPPE	And let off fireworks on the Grand Canal, and engage all the gondolas for the occasion—
MARCO	And scramble money on the Rialto among the gondoliers.
GIUSEPPE	Such a king would be a blessing to his people, and if I were a king, that is the sort of king I would be.
MARCO	And so would I!
DON AL.	Come, I'm glad to find your objections are not insuperable.
MAR. & GIU.	Oh, they're not insuperable.
GIA. & TESSA	No, they're not insuperable.

(To the right of the GIUSEPPE/MARCO/TESSA/GIANETTA lines, a brace marks them as:) Together

GIUSEPPE	Besides, we are open to conviction.
GIANETTA	Yes; they are open to conviction.
TESSA	Oh! they've often been convicted.
GIUSEPPE	Our views may have been hastily formed on insufficient grounds. They may be crude, ill-digested, erroneous. I've a very poor opinion of the politician who is not open to conviction.
TESSA	*(To GIANETTA)* Oh, he's a fine fellow!
GIANETTA	Yes, that's the sort of politician for *my* money!
DON AL.	Then we'll consider it settled. Now, as the country is in a state of insurrection, it is absolutely necessary that you should assume the reins of Government at once; and, until it is ascertained which of you is to be king, I have arranged that you will reign jointly, so that no question can arise hereafter as to the validity of any of your acts.
MARCO	As one individual?
DON AL.	As one individual.
GIUSEPPE	*(linking himself with MARCO)* Like this?
DON AL.	Something like that.
MARCO	And we may take our friends with us, and give them places about the Court?
DON AL.	Undoubtedly. That's always done!
MARCO	I'm convinced!
GIUSEPPE	So am I!
TESSA	Then the sooner we're off the better.
GIANETTA	We'll just run home and pack up a few things *(going)* —
DON AL.	Stop, stop—that won't do at all—ladies are not admitted.
ALL	What!
DON AL.	Not admitted. Not at present. Afterwards, perhaps. We'll see.
GIUSEPPE	Why, you don't mean to say you are going to separate us from our wives?
DON AL.	*(aside)* This is very awkward. *(Aloud)* Only for a time—a few months. After all, what is a few months?
TESSA	But we've only been married half an hour!
Music No. 10	FINALE, ACT I: SONG—GIANETTA "Kind Sir, You Cannot Have The Heart"
GIANETTA	Kind sir, you cannot have the heart our lives to part From those to whom an hour ago we were united!

GIANETTA
(Contd.)
	Before our flowing hopes you stem, ah, look at them,
	And pause before you deal this blow, all uninvited!
	You men can never understand that heart and hand
	Cannot be separated when we go a-yearning;
	You see, you've only women's eyes to idolize
	And only women's hearts, poor men, to set *you* burning!
	Ah me, you men will never understand that woman's heart is one with
	    woman's hand!
	
	Some kind of charm you seem to find in womankind—
	Some source of unexplain'd delight (unless you're jesting),
	But what attracts you, I confess, I cannot guess;
	To me a woman's face is quite uninteresting!
	If from my sister I were torn it could be borne—
	I should, no doubt, be horrified, but I could bear it; *(weeps)*
	But Marco's quite another thing—he is my King,
	He has my heart and none beside shall ever share it!
	Ah me, you men will never understand that woman's heart is one with
	    woman's hand!

RECITATIVE—DON ALHAMBRA

DON AL.	Do not give way to this uncalled-for grief, Your separation will be very brief. To ascertain which is the King And which the other, To Barataria's Court I'll bring His foster-mother; Her former nurseling to declare She'll be delighted. That settled, let each happy pair Be reunited.
MAR., GIU., GIA. & TESSA	Viva! His argument is strong! Viva! We'll not be parted long! Viva! It will be settled soon Viva! Then comes our honeymoon! Viva! Viva! Viva!

(Exit DON ALHAMBRA)

QUARTET—(Marco, Giuseppe, Gianetta, Tessa)

"Then One Of Us"

GIANETTA	Then one of us will be a Queen, And sit on a golden throne, With a crown instead Of a hat on her head, And diamonds all her own! With a beautiful robe of gold and green, I've always understood; I wonder whether She'd wear a feather? I rather think she should!
ALL	Oh, 'tis a glorious thing, I ween, To be a regular Royal Queen! No half-and-half affair, I mean No half-and-half affair, But a right-down regular, regular, regular, regular Royal Queen!

MARCO	She'll drive about in a carriage and pair,
	With the King on her left-hand side,
	And a milkwhite horse,
	As a matter of course!
	Whenever she wants to ride!
	With beautiful silver shoes to wear
	Upon her dainty feet;
	With endless stocks
	Of beautiful frocks
	And as much as she wants to eat!
ALL	Oh, 'tis a glorious thing, I ween,
	To be a regular Royal Queen!
	No half-and-half affair, I mean
	No half-and-half affair,
	But a right-down regular, regular, regular, regular Royal Queen!
TESSA	Whenever she condescends to walk,
	Be sure she'll shine at that,
	With her haughty stare
	And her nose in the air,
	Like a well-born aristocrat!
	At elegant high society talk
	She'll bear away the bell,
	With her "How de do?"
	And her "How are you?"
	And "I trust I see you well!"
ALL	Oh, 'tis a glorious thing, I ween,
	To be a regular Royal Queen!
	No half-and-half affair, I mean
	No half-and-half affair,
	But a right-down regular, regular, regular, regular Royal Queen!
GIUSEPPE	And noble lords will scrape and bow,
	And double themselves in two,
	And open their eyes
	In blank surprise
	At whatever she likes to do.
	And ev'rybody will roundly vow
	She's fair as flow'rs in May,
	And say, "How clever!"
	At whatsoever
	She condescends to say!
ALL	Oh! 'tis a glorious thing, I ween,
	To be a regular Royal Queen—
	No half-and-half affair, I mean
	No half-and-half affair,
	But a right-down regular, regular, regular, regular Royal Queen!
	Oh! 'tis a glorious thing, I ween
	To be a regular Royal Queen,
	A right-down regular Royal, Royal Queen!

(Dance)
(Enter chorus of Gondoliers and Contadine)

CHORUS	Now, pray, what is the cause of this remarkable hilarity?
	This sudden ebullition of unmitigated jollity?
	Has anybody bless'd you with a sample of his charity?
	Or have you been adopted by a gentleman of quality?

MARCO	Replying we
GIUSEPPE	sing As
MARCO	one indi-
GIUSEPPE	-vidual, As I
MARCO	find I'm a
GIUSEPPE	King To my
MARCO	kingdom I
GIUSEPPE	bid you all. I'm a-
MARCO	-ware you ob-
GIUSEPPE	-ject To pa-
MARCO	-vilions and
GIUSEPPE	palaces, But you'll
MARCO	find I re-
GIUSEPPE	-spect Your Re-
MARCO	-publican
GIUSEPPE	fallacies, You'll
MARCO	find I re-
GIUSEPPE	-spect Your Re-
MARCO	-publican
GIUSEPPE	fallacies

CHORUS
As they know we object to pavilions and palaces,
How can they respect our Republican fallacies?

MARCO
For ev'ry one who feels inclined,
Some post we undertake to find
Congenial with his frame of mind—
And all shall equal be.

GIUSEPPE
The Chancellor in his peruke—
The Earl, the Marquis, and the Dook,
The Groom, the Butler, and the Cook—
They all shall equal be!

MARCO
The Aristocrat who banks with Coutts,
The Aristocrat who hunts and shoots,
The Aristocrat who cleans our boots—
They all shall equal be!

GIUSEPPE
The Noble Lord who rules the State—
The Noble Lord who cleans the plate—

MARCO
The Noble Lord who scrubs the grate—
They all shall equal be!

GIUSEPPE
The Lord High Bishop orthodox—
The Lord High Coachman on the box—

MARCO
The Lord High Vagabond in the stocks—
They all shall equal be!

BOTH
For ev'ry one who feels inclined,
Some post we undertake to find
Congenial with his frame of mind,
Congenial with his frame of mind,
And all shall equal be.
Sing high, sing low, wherever they go,
Sing high, sing low, wherever they go,
Wherever they go, wherever they go,
They all shall equal be.

CHORUS

Sing high, sing low, wherever they go,
Sing high, sing low, wherever they go,
Wherever they go, wherever they go,
They all shall equal be.

GIRLS

The Earl, the
Marquis,
and the
Dook, The
Groom, the
Butler,
and the
Cook, The
Aristo-
crat who
banks with
Coutts, The
Aristo-
crat who
cleans the
boots, The
Noble
Lord who
rules the
State, The
Noble
Lord who
scrubs the
grate. The
Lord high
Bishop
ortho-
dox, The
Vagabond
in the
stocks—

MEN

The Earl,
the
Mar-
quis,
and
the
Dook,
the
Groom,
the
But-
ler,
and
the
Cook,
The
No-
ble
Lord
who
rules
the
State,
The
No-
ble
Lord
who
scrubs
the
grate—

CHORUS

For ev'ryone who feels inclined,
Some post they undertake to find,
Congenial with his frame of mind,
Congenial with his frame of mind,
And all shall equal be!
Then hail! O King, whichever you may be,
To you we sing, but do not bend the knee.
Then hail! hail! O King.
Hail! O King, Hail! O King!

MAR. & GIUS.
(Recitative)

Come, let's away—our island crown awaits me—
Conflicting feelings rend my soul apart!
The thought of Royal dignity elates me,
But leaving thee behind me breaks my heart! *(Addressing GIANETTA and TESSA)*

GIA. & TESSA
(Recitative)

Farewell my love; on board you must be getting!
But while upon the sea you gaily roam,
Remember that a heart for thee is fretting—
The tender little heart you've left at home!

GIANETTA

Now, Marco dear, my wishes hear;
While you're away

GIANETTA
(Contd.)

It's understood you will be good,
And not too gay.
To ev'ry trace of maiden grace
You will be blind,
And will not glance by any chance
On womankind!
If you are wise, you'll shut your eyes
Till we arrive
And not address a lady less
Than forty-five.
You'll please to frown on ev'ry gown
That you may see;
And, O my pet, you won't forget
You've married me!
And O my darling, O my pet,
Whatever else you may forget,
In yonder isle beyond the sea,
Do not forget, do not forget you've married me!

TESSA

You'll lay your head upon your bed
At set of sun.
You will not sing of anything
To anyone.
You'll sit and mope all day, I hope.
And shed a tear
Upon the life your little wife
Is passing here.
And if so be you think of me,
Please tell the moon!
I'll read it all in rays that fall
On the lagoon:
You'll be so kind as tell the wind
How you may be,
And send me words by little birds
To comfort me!

And O my darling, O my pet,
Whatever else you may forget,
In yonder isle beyond the sea,
Do not forget you've married me!

GIANETTA	TESSA	MARCO	GIUSEPPE
O—			
—	O—		O—
my dar-	—		—
ling,	—	O—	—
O—	my—	—	my—
—	—	my—	—
my	—	—	—
pet, What-	darling,	dar-	dar-
ever	O—	ling,	ling,
else	—		O—
you	—	O—	—
may—	my—	—	my—
—	—	my	—
for-	—	—	—
get,	pet,	pet,	pet,

ALL

In yonder isle beyond the sea,
Do ⎫
We'll ⎭ not forget,

Do ⎫ not forget ⎧ you've ⎫ married ⎧ me!
We'll ⎭   ⎩ we've ⎭   ⎩ ye!
O my darling, O my pet,
In yonder isle beyond the sea,
Do ⎫ not forget ⎧ you've ⎫ married ⎧ me!
We'll ⎭   ⎩ we've ⎭   ⎩ ye!

(During which a "Xebeque" is hauled alongside the quay)

CHORUS
Then away ⎧ they ⎫ go to an island fair
           ⎩ we ⎭
That lies in a Southern sea:
We know not where, and we don't much care
Wherever that isle may be

THE MEN
(hauling on boat)
One, two, three, Haul!
One, two, three, Haul!
One, two, three, Haul!
With a will!

ALL
When the breezes are blowing
The ship will be going,
When they don't ⎧ they will ⎫ all stand still!
            ⎩ we shall ⎭
Then away ⎧ they ⎫ go to an island fair,
           ⎩ we ⎭
We know not where, and we don't much care,
Wherever that isle may be.

GIANETTA	TESSA	MARCO	GIUSEPPE	CHORUS
		Away we go		
		To a balmy		
		isle,		
Away,	Away,		Away,	
				Away,
away	away		away	
they go	they go		we go	away,
		Where the		
		roses blow		
		All the		
		win-		
A—	A—	—	Where	
—	—	ter	the	
way, —	way, —	while, —	ro-	
—	—		ses	A-
		Ro-	blow	way,
a-	a-	—	All the	
way. —	way, —	—	win-	
—	—	ses	ter	a-
		blow,	while,	way,
		a-		
		way where—		where
		—		ro-
		the		—
		roses—		ses
		—		blow,
		blow—		
		—		All
all—		All—		win-
the		the		

33

GIANETTA (Contd.)	TESSA (Contd.)	MARCO (Contd.)	GIUSEPPE (Contd.)	CHORUS (Contd.)
win-	Where—	win-	Where—	ter
ter—	—	ter—	—	while,
—	—	—	—	
while, —	—	while, —	—	Where —
—	the—	—	the—	—
Where—	—	Where—	—	—
the	ro-	the	ro-	—
ro-	—	ro-	—	the—
ses	ses—	ses	ses—	—
blow! —	—	blow! —	—	ro-
—	blow—	—	blow—	—
—	—	—	—	ses—
—	All—	—	All—	—
—	—	—	—	blow! —
—	winter while.	—	winter while.	—

ALL

(hoisting sail)

Then away {they / we} go to an island fair
That lies in a Southern sea;
Then away {they / we} go to an island fair;
Then away, then away, then away,
Then away, away!

(The men embark on the "Xebeque". MARCO and GIUSEPPE embracing GIANETTA and TESSA. The girls wave a farewell to the men as the curtain falls.)

END OF ACT I

ACT II

scene—*Pavilion in the Court of Barataria. MARCO and GIUSEPPE, magnificently dressed, are seated on two thrones, occupied in cleaning the crown and the sceptre. The Gondoliers are discovered, dressed, some as courtiers, officers of rank etc., and others as private soldiers and servants of various degrees. All are enjoying themselves without reference to social distinctions—some playing cards, others throwing dice, some reading, others playing cup and ball, "morra" etc.*

Music No. 1	CHORUS *of* MEN *with* MARCO *and* GIUSEPPE "Of Happiness The Very Pith"
ALL	Of happiness the very pith in Barataria you may see: A monarchy that's tempered with Republican Equality.
BASSES	This form of government we find The beau-ideal of its kind—
TENORS	A despotism strict, combined With absolute equality! With absolute equality!
ALL	Of happiness the very pith in Barataria you may see: A monarchy that's tempered with Republican Equality! Republican Equality!
MAR. & GIUS.	Two kings, of undue pride bereft, who act in perfect unity, Whom you can order right and left with absolute impunity, Who put their subjects at their ease By doing all they can to please! And thus, to earn their bread-and-cheese, Seize ev'ry opportunity. And thus, to earn their bread-and-cheese, Seize ev'ry opportunity. Ah! we act in perfect unity, Ah! we act in perfect unity!
ALL	Of happiness the very pith in Barataria you may see: A monarchy that's tempered with Republican Equality! Republican Equality, tempered with Equality!
MARCO	Gentlemen, we are much obliged to you for your expressions of satisfaction and good feeling—I say, we are much obliged to you for your expressions of satisfaction and good feeling.
ALL	We heard you.
MARCO	We are delighted, at any time, to fall in with sentiments so charmingly expressed.
ALL	That's all right.
GIUSEPPE	At the same time there is just one little grievance that we should like to ventilate.
ALL *(angrily)*	What?
GIUSEPPE	Don't be alarmed—it's not serious. It is arranged that, until it is decided which of us is the actual King, we are to act as one person.
GIORGIO	Exactly.

35

GIUSEPPE	Now, although we act as *one* person, we are, in point of fact, *two* persons.
ANNIBALE	Ah, I don't think we can go into that. It is a legal fiction, and legal fictions are solemn things. Situated as we are, we can't recognize two independent responsibilities.
GIUSEPPE	No; but you can recognize two independent appetites. It's all very well to say we act as one person, but when you supply us with only one ration between us, I should describe it as a legal fiction carried a little too far.
ANNIBALE	It's rather a nice point. I don't like to express an opinion off-hand. Suppose we reserve it for argument before the full Court.
MARCO	Yes; but what are we to do in the meantime?
MAR. & GIUS.	We want our tea.
ANNIBALE	I think we may make an interim order for double rations on their Majesties entering into the usual undertaking to indemnify in the event of an adverse decision?
GIORGIO	That, I think, will meet the case. But you must work hard—stick to it—nothing like work.
GIUSEPPE	Oh, certainly. We quite understand that a man who holds the magnificent position of King should do something to justify it. We are called "Your Majesty", we are allowed to buy ourselves magnificent clothes, our subjects frequently nod to us in the streets, the sentries always return our salutes, and we enjoy the inestimable privilege of heading the subscription lists to all the principal charities. In return for these advantages the least we can do is to make ourselves useful about the Palace.
Music No. 2	SONG—GIUSEPPE (*with* Chorus) "Rising Early In The Morning"
GIUSEPPE	Rising early in the morning, we proceed to light the fire, Then our Majesty adorning in its work-a-day attire, We embark without delay on the duties of the day. First, we polish off some batches of political despatches, And foreign politicians circumvent; Then, if bus'ness isn't heavy, we may hold a Royal *levée*, Or ratify some Acts of Parliament. Then we probably review the household troops— With the usual "Shalloo humps!" and "Shalloo hoops!" Or receive with ceremonial and state An interesting Eastern potentate. After that we generally go and dress our private *valet*— (It's rather nervous duty—he's a touchy little man)— Write some letters literary for our private secretary— He is shaky in his spelling, so we help him if we can. Then, in view of cravings inner, we go down and order dinner; Then we polish the Regalia and the Coronation Plate— Spend an hour in titivating all our Gentlemen-in-Waiting; Or we run on little errands for the Ministers of State. Oh, philosophers may sing Of the troubles of a King; Yet the duties are delightful and the privileges great; But the privilege and pleasure That we treasure beyond measure Is to run on little errands for the Ministers of State.

CHORUS	Oh! Philosophers may sing, Of the troubles of a King; Yet the duties are delightful and the privileges great; But the privilege and pleasure That we treasure beyond measure Is to run on little errands for the Ministers of State.
GIUSEPPE	After luncheon (making merry On a bun and glass of sherry), If we've nothing in particular to do, We may make a Proclamation Or receive a Deputation— Then we possibly create a Peer or two. Then we help a fellow-creature on his path With the Garter, or the Thistle, or the Bath. Or we dress and toddle off in semi-State To a festival, a function, or a *fête*. Then we go and stand as sentry At the Palace (private entry), Marching hither, marching thither, up and down and to and fro, While the warrior on duty Goes in search of beer and beauty (And it generally happens that he hasn't far to go). He relieves us, if he's able, Just in time to lay the table, Then we dine and serve the coffee, and at half-past twelve or one, With a pleasure that's emphatic, We retire to our attic With the gratifying feeling that our duty has been done! Oh, philosophers may sing Of the troubles of a King; But of pleasures there are many and of worries there are none, And the culminating pleasure That we treasure beyond measure Is the gratifying feeling that our duty has been done!
CHORUS	Oh! Philosophers may sing, Of the troubles of a King; But of pleasures there are many and of worries there are none, And the culminating pleasure That we treasure beyond measure Is the gratifying feeling that our duty has been done!

(Exeunt all but MARCO and GIUSEPPE)

GIUSEPPE	Yet it really is a very pleasant existence. They're all so singularly kind and considerate. You don't find them wanting to do this, or wanting to do that, or saying "It's my turn now". No, they let us have all the fun ourselves, and never seem to grudge it.
MARCO	It makes one feel quite selfish. It almost seems like taking advantage of their good nature.
GIUSEPPE	How nice they were about the double rations.
MARCO	Most considerate. Ah! there's only one thing wanting to make us thoroughly comfortable.
GIUSEPPE	And that is?

MARCO	The dear little wives we left behind us three months ago.
GIUSEPPE	Yes, it *is* dull without female society. We can do without everything else, but we can't do without that.
MARCO	And if we have that in perfection, we have everything. There is only one recipe for perfect happiness.

Music No. 3
> SONG—(Marco)
> "Take A Pair Of Sparkling Eyes"

MARCO
Take a pair of sparkling eyes,
Hidden, ever and anon,
In a merciful eclipse—
Do not heed their mild surprise—
Having pass'd the Rubicon.
Take a pair of rosy lips;
Take a figure trimly plann'd—
Such as admiration whets
(Be particular in this);
Take a tender little hand,
Fring'd with dainty fingerettes,
Press it, press it—in parenthesis—
Ah! Take all these, you lucky man—
Take and keep them, if you can, if you can!
Take all these, you lucky man,
Take and keep them, if you can,
If you can!

Take a pretty little cot.
Quite a miniature affair—
Hung about with trellis'd vine,
Furnish it upon the spot
With the treasures rich and rare
I've endeavour'd to define.
Live to love and love to live—
You will ripen at your ease,
Growing on the sunny side—
Fate has nothing more to give.
You're a dainty man to please
If you're not satisfied, not satisfied,
Ah! Take my counsel, happy man;
Act upon it, if you can, if you can!
Take my counsel, happy man;
Act upon it, if you can, if you can!
Take my counsel, happy man;
Act upon it if you can.
If you can, if you can.
Act upon it if you can, happy man, if you can!

> *(Enter Chorus of Contadine, running in, led by FIAMETTA and VITTORIA. They are met by all the ex-Gondoliers, who welcome them heartily)*

Music No. 4
> SCENA—Chorus *of* Girls, Quartet, Duet *and* Chorus
> "Here We Are At The Risk"

CHORUS (Girls)
Here we are, at the risk of our lives,
From ever so far, and we've brought your wives—

CHORUS (Girls) *(Contd.)*	And to that end we've cross'd the main, And don't intend to return again! To that end we've cross'd the main, And don't intend to return again! Here we are, at risk of our lives, And we've brought, we've brought your wives. Here we are, at the risk of our lives, And we've brought your wives, And to that end, to that end, We've cross'd the main, And we don't, don't intend to return again!
FIAMETTA	Though obedience is strong, curiosity's stronger— We waited for long, till we couldn't wait longer.
VITTORIA	It's imprudent, we know, but without your society Existence was slow, and we wanted variety—
BOTH	Existence was slow, and we wanted variety, Yes, we wanted variety.
ALL	So here we are, at the risk of our lives, And we've brought your wives— And to that end, to that end, we've cross'd the main, And don't, don't intend to return again!

(Enter GIANETTA and TESSA. They rush to the arms of MARCO and GIUSEPPE)

GIUSEPPE	Tessa!
TESSA	Giuseppe!
GIANETTA	Marco!
MARCO	Gianetta!

Embrace

TESSA	After sailing to this island—
GIANETTA	Tossing in a manner frightful,
TESSA	We are all once more on dry land—
GIANETTA	And we find the change delightful,
TESSA	As at home we've been remaining— We've not seen you both for ages,
GIANETTA	Tell me, are you fond of reigning?— How's the food, and what's the wages?
TESSA	Does your new employment please ye?—
GIANETTA	How does Royalizing strike you?
TESSA	Is it difficult or easy?—
GIANETTA	Do you think your subjects like you?
TESSA	I am anxious to elicit, Is it plain and easy steering?

GIANETTA	Take it altogether, is it— Better fun than gondoliering?
BOTH	We shall both go on requesting, Till you tell us, never doubt it, Ev'rything is interesting, Tell us, tell us all about it!
CHORUS	They will both go on requesting, Till you tell them, never doubt it, Ev'rything is interesting, Tell us, tell us all about it!
TESSA	Is the populace exacting?
GIANETTA	Do they keep you at a distance?
TESSA	All unaided are you acting,
GIANETTA	Or do they provide assistance?
TESSA	When you're busy, have you got to Get up early in the morning?
GIANETTA	If you do what you ought not to, Do they give the usual warning?
TESSA	With a horse do they equip you?
GIANETTA	Lots of trumpeting and drumming?
TESSA	Do the Royal tradesmen tip you?
GIANETTA	Ain't the livery becoming!
TESSA	Does your human being inner Feed on ev'rything that nice is?
GIANETTA	Do they give you wine for dinner? Peaches, sugar-plums, and ices?
BOTH	We shall both go on requesting Till you tell us, never doubt it; Ev'rything is interesting, Tell us, tell us all about it!
CHORUS	They will both go on requesting, Till you tell them, never doubt it, Ev'rything is interesting, Tell us, tell us all about it!

GIANETTA & TESSA
We shall
both go on requesting,
Till you tell us, never doubt it,
Ev'rything is interesting,
Tell us, tell us all about it!
Ev'rything is interesting,
Tell us, tell us all about it!
Tell us
all,

CHORUS
They'll go on requesting,
Till you tell them, never doubt it,
Ev'rything is interesting,
Tell us, tell us all about it!
Ev'rything is interesting,
Tell us, tell us all about it!
Ev'ry-
thing is interesting,

GIANETTA & TESSA *(Contd.)*	**CHORUS** *(Contd.)*
yes,	Ev'ry-
all,	thing is interesting,
yes,	Tell us,
tell	tell us
us,	all a-
tell	bout it!
us,	Tell us,
tell	tell us
us,	all a-
tell	bout it,
us	Tell us,
all,	tell us
all about it!	all about it!

MARCO   This is indeed a most delightful surprise!

TESSA   Yes, we thought you'd like it. You see, it was like this: After you left we felt very dull and mopey, and the days crawled by, and you never wrote; so at last I said to Gianetta, "I can't stand this any longer; those two poor Monarchs haven't got anyone to mend their stockings or sew on their buttons or patch their clothes—at least, I hope they haven't—let us all pack up a change and go and see how they're getting on." And she said "Done", and they all said "Done"; and we asked old Giacopo to lend us his boat, and *he* said "Done", and we've crossed the sea, and, thank goodness, *that's* done; and here we are, and— and— *I've* done!

GIANETTA   And now—which of you is King?

TESSA   And which of us is Queen?

GIUSEPPE   That we shan't know until Nurse turns up. But never mind that—the question is, how shall we celebrate the commencement of our honeymoon? Gentlemen, will you allow us to offer you a magnificent banquet?

ALL   We will!

GIUSEPPE   Thanks very much; and, ladies, what do you say to a dance?

TESSA   A banquet *and* a dance! Oh, it's too much happiness!

Music No. 5   CHORUS *and* DANCE
"Dance A Cachucha"

CHORUS   Dance a cachucha, fandango, bolero,
Xeres we'll drink—Manzanilla, Montero—
Wine, when it runs in abundance, enhances
The reckless delight of that wildest of dances!

GIRLS   To the pretty pitter-pitter-patter,
And the clitter-clitter-clitter-clatter-
Clitter-clitter-clatter,
Pitter-pitter-patter,
Clitter-clitter-clatter,
Clitter-clitter,

GIRLS	**MEN**
Clatter pretty pitter-pitter-patter,	To the pretty pitter-pitter-patter,
And the clitter-clitter-clitter-clatter—	And the clitter-clitter-clitter-clatter—

GIRLS	Pitter-pitter-pitter, Patter-patter-patter, patter We'll dance,
ALL	Old Xeres we'll drink—Manzanilla, Montero; For wine, when it runs in abundance, enhances The reckless delight of that wildest of dances! That wildest of dances, The reckless delight! Dance a cachucha, fandango, bolero, Xeres we'll drink—Manzanilla, Montero— Wine, when it runs in abundance, enhances The reckless delight of that wildest of dances! Old Xeres we'll drink—Manzanilla, Montero, For wine, when it runs in abundance enhances The reckless delight of that wildest of dances, The reckless delight of that wildest of dances!

CACHUCHA

(The dance is interrupted by the unexpected appearance of DON ALHAMBRA, who looks on with astonishment. MARCO and GIUSEPPE appear embarrassed. The others run off, except Drummer-Boy, who is driven off by DON ALHAMBRA)

DON AL.	Good evening. Fancy ball?
GIUSEPPE	No, not exactly. A little friendly dance. That's all. Sorry you're late.
DON AL.	But I saw a groom dancing, and a footman!
MARCO	Yes. That's the Lord High Footman.
DON AL.	And, dear me, a common little drummer-boy!
GIUSEPPE	Oh no! That's the Lord High Drummer-boy.
DON AL.	But surely, surely the servants'-hall is the place for these gentry?
GIUSEPPE	Oh dear no! *We* have appropriated the servants'-hall. It's the Royal Apartment, and accessible only by tickets obtainable at the Lord Chamberlain's office.
MARCO	We really must have some place that we can call our own.
DON AL.	*(puzzled)* I'm afraid I'm not quite equal to the intellectual pressure of the conversation.
GIUSEPPE	You see, the Monarchy has been re-modelled on Republican principles.
DON AL.	What!
GIUSEPPE	All departments rank equally, and everybody is at the head of his department.
DON AL.	I see.
MARCO	I'm afraid you're annoyed.
DON AL.	No, I won't say that. It's not quite what I expected.

GIUSEPPE	I'm awfully sorry.
MARCO	So am I.
GIUSEPPE	By-the-bye, can I offer you anything after your voyage? A plate of macaroni and a rusk?
DON AL.	*(pre-occupied)* No, no—nothing—nothing.
GIUSEPPE	Obliged to be careful?
DON AL.	Yes—gout. You see, in every Court there are distinctions that must be observed.
GIUSEPPE	*(puzzled)* There are, are there?
DON AL.	Why, of course. For instance, you wouldn't have a Lord High Chancellor playing leapfrog with his own cook.
MARCO	Why not?
DON AL.	Why not? Because a Lord High Chancellor is a personage of great dignity, who should never, under any circumstances, place himself in the position of being told to tuck in his tuppeny, except by noblemen of his own rank. A Lord High Archbishop, for instance, might tell a Lord High Chancellor to tuck in his tuppeny, but certainly not a cook, gentlemen—certainly not a cook.
GIUSEPPE	Not even a Lord High Cook?
DON AL.	My good friend, that is a rank that is not recognized at the Lord Chamberlain's office. No, no, it won't do. I'll give you an instance in which the experiment was tried.
Music No. 6	SONG—DON ALHAMBRA (*with* Marco *and* Giuseppe) "There Lived A King"
DON AL.	There lived a King, as I've been told, In the wonder-working days of old, When hearts were twice as good as gold, And twenty times as mellow. Good-temper triumphed in his face, And in his heart he found a place For all the erring human race And ev'ry wretched fellow. When he had Rhenish wine to drink It made him very sad to think That some, at junket or at jink, Must be content with toddy.
MAR. & GIUS.	With toddy, must be content with toddy.
DON AL.	He wished all men as rich as he (And he was rich as rich could be), So to the top of ev'ry tree Promoted ev'rybody.
MAR. & GIUS.	Now, that's the kind of King for me— He wished all men as rich as he, So to the top of ev'ry tree Promoted ev'rybody!

43

DON AL.	Lord Chancellors were cheap as sprats, And Bishops in their shovel hats Were plentiful as tabby cats— In point of fact, too many, Ambassadors cropped up like hay, Prime Ministers and such as they Grew like asparagus in May, And Dukes were three a penny. On ev'ry side Field Marshals gleam'd, Small beer were Lords Lieutenant deem'd, With Admirals the ocean teem'd All round his wide dominions.
MAR. & GIUS.	With Admirals around his wide dominions.
DON AL.	And Party Leaders you might meet In twos and threes in ev'ry street Maintaining, with no little heat, Their various opinions.
MAR. & GIUS.	Now that's a sight you couldn't beat— Two Party Leaders in each street Maintaining, with no little heat, Their various opinions.
DON AL.	That King, although no one denies His heart was of abnormal size, Yet he'd have acted otherwise If he had been acuter. The end is easily foretold, When ev'ry blessed thing you hold Is made of silver, or of gold, You long for simple pewter. When you have nothing else to wear But cloth of gold and satins rare, For cloth of gold you cease to care— Up goes the price of shoddy.
MAR. & GIUS.	Of shoddy, up goes the price of shoddy.
DON AL.	In short, whoever you may be, To this conclusion you'll agree, When everyone is somebodee, Then no one's anybody!
MAR. & GIUS.	Now that's plain as plain can be. To this conclusion we agree—
ALL	When everyone is somebodee, Then no one's anybody!
	(GIANETTA and TESSA enter unobserved. The two girls, impelled by curiosity, remain listening at the back of the stage)
DON AL.	And now I have some important news to communicate. His Grace the Duke of Plaza-Toro, Her Grace the Duchess, and their beautiful daughter Casilda—I say their beautiful daughter Casilda—
GIUSEPPE	We heard you.
DON AL.	Have arrived at Barataria, and may be here at any moment.

MARCO	The Duke and Duchess are nothing to us.
DON AL.	But the daughter—the beautiful daughter! Aha! Oh, you're a lucky dog, one of you!
GIUSEPPE	I think you're a very incomprehensible old gentleman.
DON AL.	Not a bit. I'll explain: Many years ago when you (whichever you are) were a baby, you (whichever you are) were married to a little girl who has grown up to be the most beautiful young lady in Spain. That beautiful young lady will be here to claim you (whichever you are) in half an hour, and I congratulate that one (whichever it is) with all my heart.
MARCO	Married when a baby!
GIUSEPPE	But we were married three months ago!
DON AL.	One- of you—only one. The other (whichever it is) is an unintentional bigamist.
GIA. & TESSA	*(Coming forward)* Well, upon my word!
DON AL.	Eh? Who are these young people?
TESSA	Who are we? Why, their wives, of course. We've just arrived.
DON AL.	Their wives! O dear, this is very unfortunate! Oh dear, this complicates matters! Dear, dear, what will Her Majesty say?
GIANETTA	And do you mean to say that one of these Monarchs was already married?
TESSA	And that neither of us will be a Queen?
DON AL.	That is the idea I intended to convey. *(TESSA and GIANETTA begin to cry)*
GIUSEPPE	*(to TESSA)* Tessa, my dear, dear child—
TESSA	Get away! perhaps it's you!
MARCO	*(to GIANETTA)* My poor, poor little woman!
GIANETTA	Don't! Who knows whose husband you are?
TESSA	And pray, why didn't you tell us all about it before they left Venice?
DON AL.	Because, if I had, no earthly temptation would have induced these gentlemen to leave two such extremely fascinating and utterly irresistible little ladies!
TESSA	There's something in that.
DON AL.	I may mention that you will not be kept long in suspense, as the old lady who nursed the Royal child is at present in the Torture Chamber, waiting for me to interview her.
GIUSEPPE	Poor old girl. Hadn't you better go and put her out of her suspense?
DON AL.	Oh no—there's no hurry—she's all right. She has all the illustrated papers. However, I'll go and interrogate her, and, in the meantime, may I suggest the absolute propriety of your regarding yourselves as single young ladies.

45

DON AL. *(Contd.)*   Good evening!

(Exit DON ALHAMBRA)

GIANETTA   Well, here's a pleasant state of things!

MARCO   Delightful. One of us is married to two young ladies, and nobody knows which; and the other is married to one young lady whom nobody can identify!

GIANETTA   And one of us is married to one of you, and the other is married to nobody.

TESSA   But which of you is married to which of us, and what's to become of the other? *(About to cry)*

GIUSEPPE   It's quite simple. Observe. Two husbands have managed to acquire three wives. Three wives—two husbands. *(Reckoning up)* That's two-thirds of a husband to each wife.

TESSA   O Mount Vesuvius, here we are in arithmetic! My good sir, one can't marry a vulgar fraction!

GIUSEPPE   You've no right to call me a vulgar fraction.

MARCO   We are getting rather mixed. The situation is entangled. Let's try and comb it out.

Music No. 7   QUARTET (Marco, Giuseppe, Gianetta *and* Tessa) "In A Contemplative Fashion"

ALL FOUR   In a contemplative fashion,
And a tranquil frame of mind,
Free from ev'ry kind of passion,
Some solution let us find.
Let us grasp the situation,
Solve the complicated plot
Quiet, calm deliberation
Disentangles every knot.

TESSA

	OTHERS	In
I,		
no		a
doubt, Giusep-		con-
pe		tem-
wedded—That's,		pla-
of		tive
course,		fash-
a slice of		ion,
luck. He		And
is		a
rather dun-		tran-
der-		quil
headed, Still		frame
dis-		of
tinctly he's a		mind

46

GIANETTA	TESSA	MARCO	GIUSEPPE
	duck.	Free	Free
I,			
a		from	from
victim too	Ev-	ev-	ev-
of	'ry	'ry	'ry
Cupid, Mar-	kind	kind	kind
co	of	of	of
married—	passion,	passion,	passion,
that is			
clear. He's	Some	Some	Some
par-	so-	so-	so-
ticular-	lu-	lu-	lu-
ly	tion	tion	tion
stupid, Still	let	let	let
dis-	us	us	us
tinctly, he's a	find.	find.	find.
dear.	Let		Let
		To	
	us	Gia-	us
Grasp	grasp	netta I	grasp
the	the	was	the
sit-	sit-	mated; I	sit-
uation,	uation,	can prove it	uation,
		in a	
Solve	Solve	trice, Though	Solve
the	the	her	the
com-	com-	charms are o-	com-
pli-	pli-	ver-	pli-
ca-	ca-	rated, Still	ca-
ted plot,	ted plot,	I own she's	ted plot,
		rather	
Qui-	Qui-	nice.	
			I
et,	et,		to
calm	calm	Calm	Tessa, wil-
de-	de-	de-	ly-
li-	li-	li-	nilly, All
beration,	beration,	beration,	at once a
			victim
Dis-	Dis-	Dis-	fell. She
en-	en-	en-	is
tan-	tan-	tan-	what is called
gles	gles	gles	a
ev-	ev-	ev-	silly, Still
'ry	'ry	'ry	she
knot!	knot!	knot!	answers
			pretty well. She's a
			silly, still she
			answers pretty well.
In	In		In
		Now	
a	a	when	a
con-	con-	we were pret-	con-
tem-	tem-	ty	tem-
pla-	pla-	babies, Some	pla-
tive fashion,	tive fashion,	one married	tive fashion,
		us, that's	
	And	clear-	And
	a		a

GIANETTA (Contd.)	TESSA (Contd.)	MARCO (Contd.)	GIUSEPPE (Contd.)
And if I can catch her	tran- quil	tran- quil	tran- quil
I'll pinch her and scratch her,	frame of	frame of	frame of
And send her away with a flea in her ear.	mind, Free	mind, Free	mind,
	from	from	He, whom that young la- dy married, To receive her can't re- fuse.
Ev- 'ry kind of passion,	ev- 'ry kind of passion,	ev- 'ry kind of passion,	
Some so-		Some so-	
lu- tion	If I overtake her	lu- tion	-lu- tion
let us	I'll warrant I'll make her	let us	let us
find.	To shake in her aristo- cratical shoes!	find.	find.
		Let	Let
If she married your Giu- seppe, You and he will have to part—	grasp the sit- uation,	us grasp the sit- uation,	us grasp the sit- uation,
		Solve the	Solve the
com- pli-	If I have to do it	com- pli-	com- pli-
ca- ted	I'll warrant she'll rue it—	ca- ted	ca- ted
plot, Qui- et, calm	I'll teach her to marry the man of my heart!	plot, Qui- et, calm	plot, Qui- et, calm
de- li- beration	If she married Mes- ser Marco You're a spinster,	de- li- beration	de- li- beration
		Dis- en-	Dis- en-
No matter, no matter,	tan- gles	tan- gles	tan- gles
If I can get at her	ev- 'ry	ev- 'ry	ev- 'ry

GIANETTA	TESSA	MARCO	GIUSEPPE
(Contd.)	*(Contd.)*	*(Contd.)*	*(Contd.)*
I			
doubt if her	knot!	knot!	knot!
mother will know her again!			
	If		
	I have		
No	to		
matter, no	do it I'll	To Gia-	
matter, If	warrant she'll	netta	
I can get	rue it—I'll	I was	I to
at her I	teach her to	mated;	Tessa,
doubt if her	marry the	I can	willy
mother will	man of my	prove it	nilly,
know her a-	heart! If	in a	All at
gain! No	I have to	trice:	once a
matter, no	do it I'll	'Tho her	victim
matter, If	warrant she'll	charms are	fell.
I can get	rue it—I'll	over-	She is
at her I	teach her to	rated	what is
doubt if her	marry the	Still I	call'd a
mother will	man of my	own she's	silly,
know her a-	heart! I'll	rather	call'd a
gain! No	teach her, I'll	nice, She's	silly,
matter, no	teach her, I'll	rather,	silly,
matter, no	teach her, I'll	rather,	silly,
matter, no	teach her, I'll	rather,	silly,
matter, no	teach her, I'll	rather,	silly,
matter, no	teach her, I'll	rather,	still she
matter, no	teach her, I'll	rather,	answers
matter, no	teach her, I'll	rather,	pretty
matter!	teach her!	nice.	well.

ALL FOUR Quiet, calm deliberation
Disentangles ev'ry knot!

(Exeunt, pondering)
MARCH. Enter procession of Retainers, heralding the approach of DUKE, DUCHESS and CASILDA. All three are now dressed with the utmost magnificence.

Music No. 8 CHORUS of MEN (*with* Duke *and* Duchess)
"With Ducal Pomp And Ducal Pride"

CHORUS With ducal pomp and ducal pride
(Announce these comers,
O ye kettle-drummers!)
Comes Barataria's high-born bride,
(Ye sounding cymbals clang!)
She comes to claim the Royal hand—
(Proclaim their Graces,
O ye double basses!)
Of the King who rules this goodly land.
(Ye brazen brasses bang!)
She comes to claim the Royal hand,
(Ye brazen brasses bang!)

DUKE This polite attention touches
Heart of Duke

DUCHESS	And heart of Duchess, Who resign their pet!
DUKE	With profound regret.
DUCHESS	She of beauty was a model
DUKE	When a tiny, tiddle-toddle, And at twenty-one,
DUCHESS	She's excelled by none!
DUKE	At twenty-one,
DUCHESS	She's excelled by none, At twenty-one
DUKE	She's excelled by none.
CHORUS	She comes to claim the Royal hand (Proclaim their graces, O ye double-basses! Of the King who rules this goodly land. Ye brazen brasses bang!)
DUKE	*(to his attendants)* Be good enough to inform His Majesty that His Grace the Duke of Plaza-Toro, Limited, has arrived, and begs—
CASILDA	Desires—
DUCHESS	Demands—
DUKE	And demands an audience. *(Exeunt attendants)* And now, my child, prepare to receive the husband to whom you were united under such interesting and romantic circumstances.
CASILDA	But which is it? There are two of them!
DUKE	It is true that at present His Majesty is a double gentleman; but as soon as the circumstances of his marriage are ascertained, he will, *ipso facto*, boil down to a single gentleman—thus presenting a unique example of an individual who becomes a single man and a married man by the same operation.
DUCHESS	*(severely)* I have known instances in which the characteristics of both conditions existed concurrently in the same individual.
DUKE	Ah, he couldn't have been a Plaza-Toro.
DUCHESS	Oh! couldn't he, though!
CASILDA	Well, whatever happens, I shall, of course, be a dutiful wife, but I can never love my husband.
DUKE	I don't know. It's extraordinary what unprepossessing people one can love if one gives one's mind to it.
DUCHESS	I loved your father.
DUKE	My love—that remark is a little hard, I think? Rather cruel perhaps? Somewhat uncalled for, I venture to believe?

DUCHESS   It was very difficult, my dear; but I said to myself, "That man is a Duke, and I *will* love him". Several of my relations bet I couldn't, but I did—desperately!

Music No. 9   SONG —DUCHESS
"On The Day When I Was Wedded"

DUCHESS   On the day when I was wedded
To your admirable sire,
I acknowledge that I dreaded
An explosion of his ire.
I was overcome with panic—
For his temper was volcanic,
And I didn't dare revolt,
For I fear'd a thunderbolt!
I was always very wary,
For his fury was ecstatic—
His refined vocabulary
Most unpleasantly emphatic.
To the thunder of this Tartar
I knock'd under like a martyr;
When intently he was fuming,
I was gently unassuming—
When reviling me completely,
I was smiling very sweetly:
I was smiling very sweetly,
Very sweetly.
Giving him the very best, and getting back the very worst—
That is how I tried to tame your great progenitor—at first!
Giving him the very best, and getting back the very worst—
That is how I tried to tame your great progenitor—at first!

But I found that a reliance
On my threatening appearance.
And a resolute defiance
Of marital interference,
And a gentle intimation
Of my firm determination
To see what I could do
To be wife and husband, too,
Was the only thing required
For to make his temper supple,
And you couldn't have desir'd
A more reciprocating couple
Ever willing to be wooing.
We were billing—we were cooing!
When I merely from him parted
We were nearly broken-hearted—
When in sequel reunited,
We were equally delighted.
We were equally delighted, delighted.
So with double-shotted guns and colours nail'd unto the mast,
I tam'd your insignificant progenitor—at last!
So with double-shotted guns and colours nail'd unto the mast,
I tam'd your insignificant progenitor—at last!

CASILDA   My only hope is that when my husband sees what a shady family he has married into he will repudiate the contract altogether.

51

DUKE	Shady? A nobleman shady, who is blazing in the lustre of unaccustomed pocket-money? A nobleman shady, who can look back upon ninety-five quarterings? It is not every nobleman who is ninety-five quarters in arrear—I mean, who can look back upon ninety-five of them! And this, just as I have been floated at a premium! Oh fie!
DUCHESS	Your Majesty is surely unaware that directly Your Majesty's father came before the public he was applied for over and over again.
DUKE	My dear, Her Majesty's father was in the habit of being applied for over and over again—and very urgently applied for, too—long before he was registered under the Limited Liability Act.
Music No. 10	RECITATIVE AND DUET (Duke *and* Duchess) "To Help Unhappy Commoners"
DUKE	To help unhappy commoners, and add to their enjoyment, Affords a man of noble rank congenial employment; Of our attempts we offer you examples illustrative; The work is light; and, I may add, it's most remunerative.
	Small titles and orders For Mayors and Recorders I get—and they're highly delighted—
DUCHESS	They're highly delighted!
DUKE	M.P.s baronetted, Sham Colonels gazetted, And second-rate Aldermen knighted—
DUCHESS	Yes, Aldermen knighted.
DUKE	Foundation-stone laying I find very paying: It adds a large sum to my makings—
DUCHESS	Large sum to his makings.
DUKE	At charity dinners The best of speech-spinners, I get ten per cent. on the takings—
DUCHESS	One-tenth of the takings. I present any lady Whose conduct is shady Or smacking of doubtful propriety—
DUKE	Doubtful propriety.
DUCHESS	When Virtue would quash her, I take and whitewash her, And launch her in first-rate society—
DUKE	First-rate society!
DUCHESS	I recommend acres Of clumsy dressmakers— Their fit and their finishing touches.

DUKE	Their finishing touches.
DUCHESS	A sum in addition They pay for permission To say that they make for the Duchess—
DUKE	They make for the Duchess! Those pressing prevailers, The ready-made tailors, Quote me as their great double-barrel—
DUCHESS	Their great double-barrel
DUKE	I allow them to do so, Though Robinson Crusoe Would jib at their wearing apparel!
DUCHESS	Such wearing apparel!
DUKE	I sit, by selection, Upon the direction Of several Companies bubble—
DUCHESS	All Companies bubble!
DUKE	As soon as they're floated I'm freely bank-noted— I'm pretty well paid for my trouble!
DUCHESS	He's paid for his trouble! At middle-class party I play at *ècarté*— And I'm by no means a beginner—
DUKE	*(significantly)* She's not a beginner.
DUCHESS	To one of my station The remuneration— Five guineas a night and my dinner—
DUKE	And wine with her dinner.
DUCHESS	I write letters blatant On medicines patent— And use any other you mustn't—
DUKE	Believe me, you mustn't—
DUCHESS	And vow my complexion Derives its perfection From somebody's soap—which it doesn't—
DUKE	*(significantly)* It certainly doesn't! We're ready as witness To any one's fitness To fill any place or preferment—
DUCHESS	A place or preferment. We're often in waiting At junket or *fêting* And sometimes attend an interment—

DUKE	We enjoy an interment.
BOTH	In short, if you'd kindle The spark of a swindle Lure simpletons into your clutches— Yes; into your clutches. Or hoodwink a debtor You cannot do better
DUCHESS	Than trot out a Duke or a Duchess—
DUKE	A Duke
BOTH	Or a Duchess!

(Enter MARCO and GIUSEPPE)

DUKE	Ah! Their Majesties. Your Majesty! *(Bows with great ceremony)*
MARCO	The Duke of Plaza-Toro, I believe?
DUKE	The same. *(MARCO and GIUSEPPE offer to shake hands with him. The DUKE bows ceremoniously. They endeavour to imitate him)* Allow me to present—
GIUSEPPE	The young lady one of us married?

(MARCO and GIUSEPPE offer to shake hands with her. CASILDA curtsies formally. They endeavour to imitate her)

CASILDA	Gentlemen, I am the most obedient servant of one of you. *(Aside)* Oh, Luiz!
DUKE	I am now about to address myself to the gentleman whom my daughter married; the other may allow his attention to wander if he likes, for what I am about to say does not concern him. Sir, you will find in this young lady a combination of excellences which you would search for in vain in any young lady who had not the good fortune to be my daughter. There is some little doubt as to which of you is the gentleman I am addressing, and which is the gentleman who is allowing his attention to wander; but when that doubt is solved, I shall say (still addressing the attentive gentleman), "Take her, and may she make you happier than her mother has made me."
DUCHESS	Sir!
DUKE	If possible! And now there is a little matter to which I think I am entitled to take exception. I come here in State with Her Grace the Duchess and Her Majesty, my daughter, and what do I find? Do I find, for instance, a guard of honour to receive me? No.
MAR. & GIUS.	No.
DUKE	The town illuminated? No.
MAR & GIUS.	No.
DUKE	Refreshment provided? No.
MAR. & GIUS.	No.

DUKE	A Royal salute fired? No.
MAR. & GIUS.	No.
DUKE	Triumphal arches erected? No.
MAR. & GIUS.	No.
DUKE	The bells set ringing?
MAR. & GIUS.	No.
DUKE	Yes—one—the Visitors', and I rang it myself. It is not enough! It is not enough!
GIUSEPPE	Upon my honour, I'm very sorry; but you see, I was brought up in a gondola, and my ideas of politeness are confined to taking off my cap to my passengers when they tip me.
DUCHESS	That's all very well in its way, but it is not enough.
GIUSEPPE	I'll take anything else off in reason.
DUKE	But a Royal Salute to my daughter—it costs so little.
CASILDA	Papa, I don't want a Salute.
GIUSEPPE	My dear sir, as soon as we know which of us is entitled to take that liberty she shall have as many salutes as she likes.
MARCO	As for guards of honour and triumphal arches, you don't know our people —they wouldn't stand it.
GIUSEPPE	They are very off-hand with us—very off-hand indeed.
DUKE	Oh, but you mustn't allow that—you must keep them in proper discipline, you must impress your Court with your importance. You want deport-ment—carriage—
GIUSEPPE	We've got a carriage.
DUKE	Manner—dignity. There must be a good deal of this sort of thing—*(busi-ness)*—and a little of this sort of thing—*(business)* and possibly just a *soupçon* of this sort of thing! *(business)*—and so on. Oh, it's very useful, and most effective. Just attend to me. You are a King—I am a subject. Very good.
Music No. 11	GAVOTTE (Duke, Duchess, Casilda, Marco *and* Giuseppe) "I Am A Courtier Grave And Serious"
DUKE	I am a courtier grave and serious Who is about to kiss your hand; Try to combine a pose imperious With a demeanour nobly bland.
MAR. & GIUS.	Let us combine a pose imperious With a demeanour nobly bland.

(MARCO and GIUSEPPE endeavour to carry out his instructions)

DUKE	That's, if anything, *too* unbending— Too aggressively stiff and grand;

(They suddenly modify their attitudes)

	Now to the other extreme you're tending— Don't be so deucedly condescending!
DUCH. & CAS.	Now to the other extreme you're tending— Don't be so dreadfully condescending!
MAR. & GIUS.	Oh, hard to please some noblemen seem! At first, if anything, *too* unbending; Off we go to the other extreme— Too confoundedly condescending!
DUKE	Now a gavotte perform sedately— Offer your hand with conscious pride! Take an attitude not too stately, Still sufficiently dignified.
MAR. & GIUS.	Now for an attitude not too stately, Still sufficiently dignified.

(They endeavour to carry out his instructions)

DUKE	*(beating time)* Oncely, twicely—oncely, twicely— Bow impressively ere you glide. *(They do so)* Capital both, capital both—you've caught it nicely! That is the style of thing precisely!
DUCH. & CAS.	Capital both, capital both—you've caught it nicely! This is the style of thing precisely!
MAR. & GIUS.	Oh, sweet to earn a nobleman's praise! Capital both, capital both—we've caught it nicely! Supposing he's right in what he says, This is the style of thing precisely!

CASILDA & DUCHESS	**MAR., GIUS. & DUKE**
Capital, both, capital, both—you've caught it nicely!	Ah,
	this
That is the style of thing pre-	the
cisely!	style,
That is the style of thing, the	this } is the style of thing, the that }

DUCHESS	**OTHERS**
style, the style	style
of thing precisely	of thing precisely!

(GAVOTTE. At the end exeunt DUKE and DUCHESS, leaving CASILDA with MARCO and GIUSEPPE)

GIUSEPPE	*(to MARCO)* The old birds have gone away and left the young chickens together. That's called tact.
MARCO	It's very awkward. We really ought to tell her how we are situated. It's not fair to the girl.
GIUSEPPE	Then why don't you do it?
MARCO	I'd rather not—you.

GIUSEPPE	I don't know how to begin. *(To CASILDA)* A—Madam—I—we, that is, several of us—
CASILDA	Gentlemen, I am bound to listen to you; but it is right to tell you that, not knowing I was married in infancy, I am over head and ears in love with somebody else.
GIUSEPPE	Our case exactly! *We* are over head and ears in love with somebody else! *(Enter GIANETTA and TESSA)* In point of fact, with our wives!
CASILDA	Your wives! Then you are married?
TESSA	It's not our fault.
GIANETTA	We knew nothing about it.
BOTH	We are sisters of misfortune.
CASILDA	My good girls, I don't blame you. Only before we go any further we must really arrive at some satisfactory arrangement, or we shall get hopelessly-complicated.

Music No. 12	QUINTET *and* FINALE (Marco, Giuseppe, Casilda, Gianetta, Tessa) "Here Is A Case Unprecedented!"
ALL	Here is a case unprecedented! Here are a King and Queen ill-starr'd! Ever since marriage was first invented Never was known a case so hard!
MAR. & GIUS.	I may be said to have been bisected, By a profound catastrophe!
CAS., GIA. & TESSA	Through a calamity unexpected I am divisible into three!
MAR. & GIUS.	I may be said to have been bisected!
CAS., GIA. & TESSA	I am divisible into three! Through a calamity I am divisible into three!
ALL	O moralists all, How can you call Marriage a state of unitee,

CASILDA	**GIA. & TESSA**	**MARCO**	**GIUSEPPE**
of—	Ah!		Ah!—
—	of	of	—
u-	u-	u-	u-
—	—	—	ni-
ni-	ni-	ni-	—
tee!	tee!	tee!	tee!

ALL	Moralists all, How can you call Marriage a state of unitee! Moralists all, How can you call Marriage a state of unitee!

MARCO		**OTHERS**	Call—
	Call		—

ALL marriage a state of union true,

CAS., GIA. & TESSA	**MARCO & GIUSEPPE**
One-third of myself is	When half of myself has
married to half of ye, or you!	married two thirds of ye, or you!

(Enter DON ALHAMBRA, followed by DUKE, DUCHESS, and all the Chorus)

RECITATIVE—DON ALHAMBRA

Now let the loyal lieges gather round—
The Prince's foster-mother has been found!
She will declare, to silver clarion's sound,
The rightful King—let him forthwith be crown'd!

CHORUS She will declare, to silver clarion's sound,
The rightful King—let him forthwith be crown'd!

(DON ALHAMBRA brings forward INEZ, the Prince's foster-mother)

TESSA Speak, woman, speak—

DUKE We're all attention!

GIANETTA The news we seek—

DUCHESS This moment mention.

CASILDA To us they bring—

DON AL. His foster-mother.

MARCO Is he the King?

GIUSEPPE Or this my brother?

ALL Speak, woman, speak!
Speak, woman, speak!

INEZ
(Recitative) The Royal Prince was by the King entrusted
To my fond care, ere I grew old and crusted:
When traitors came to steal his son reputed,
My own small boy I deftly substituted!
The villains fell into the trap completely—
I hid the Prince away—still sleeping sweetly;
I called him "son" with pardonable slyness—
His name, Luiz! Behold his Royal Highness!

(Sensation. LUIZ ascends the throne, crowned and robed as King)

CASILDA *(rushing to his arms)* Luiz!

LUIZ Casilda! *(Embrace)*

ALL Is this indeed the King, oh, wondrous revelation!
Oh, unexpected thing! Unlook'd-for situation!

MAR., GIA., **GIUS. & TESS.**	This statement we receive with sentiments conflicting; Our hearts rejoice and grieve, each other contradicting; To those whom we adore we can be reunited— On one point rather sore, but, on the whole, delighted!
LUIZ	When others claim'd thy dainty hand. I waited—waited—waited.
DUKE	As prudence (so I understand) dictated—tated—tated.
CASILDA	By virtue of our early vow recorded—corded—corded.
DUCHESS	Your pure and patient love is now Rewarded—warded—warded.
ALL	Then hail, O King of a Golden Land, And the high-born bride who claims his hand! The past is dead, and you gain your own, A royal crown and a golden throne!

FANFARE

(All kneel : LUIZ crowns CASILDA)

ALL	Once more *gondolieri*, both skilful and wary, Free from this quandary, contented are we. Ah! From Royalty flying, our gondolas plying And merrily crying our "*premé*" "*stali*"! Ah! So, good-bye cachucha, fandango, bolero— We'll dance a farewell to that measure— Old Xeres, adieu—Manzanilla—Montero— We leave you with feelings of pleasure! Once more *Gondolieri*, both skilful and wary, Free from this quandary, contented are we. Ah! Ah! Once more *gondolieri*, *gondolieri*, *Gondolieri*, contented are we So good-bye cachucha, fandango, bolero, We'll dance a farewell to that measure— Old Xeres, adieu, Manzanilla—Montero— We leave you with feelings of pleasure! With feelings of pleasure!

CURTAIN